Amazing Animals
Alligators and Crocodiles

Angela Royston

Published by Smart Apple Media
1980 Lookout Drive
North Mankato, MN 56003

Amazing Animals series © 2004
WEIGL PUBLISHERS INC. www.weigl.com

Library of Congress Cataloging-in-Publication
Data

Royston, Angela.
  Alligators and crocodiles / Angela Royston.
    p. cm. – (Amazing animals series)
  Summary: An introduction to the physical
features of alligators and crocodiles, their
habitat, life cycle, and relationships with other
animals, as well as conservation efforts and
related facts.
  ISBN 1-58340-225-X (Library Bound : alk.
paper)
  1. Alligators–Juvenile literature. 2.
Crocodiles–Juvenile
literature. [1. Alligators. 2. Crocodiles.] I.
Title. II. Series.
  QL666.C925 R69 2003
  597.98–dc21

2002152361

Printed in Malaysia
9 8 7 6 5 4 3 2 1

Photograph Credits
Every reasonable effort has been made
to trace ownership and to obtain permission
to reprint copyright material. The publishers
would be pleased to have any errors or
omissions brought to their attention so
that they may be corrected in
subsequent printings.

Cover: Crocodile (Dave Taylor); Warren Clark:
pages 6, 20, 21; Corel Corporation: pages 1,
4, 5, 7, 9, 10, 11, 13, 15, 17; Dave Taylor:
pages 2, 3, 8, 12, 14, 16, 18, 19, 23.

Series Editors
Diana Marshall and Jennifer Nault
Layout
Bryan Pezzi
Photo Researchers
Tina Schwartzenberger, Peggy Chan,
and Wendy Cosh

About This Book

This book tells you all about alligators and crocodiles. Find out where they live and what they eat. Discover how you can help to protect them. You can also read about them in myths and legends from around the world.

Words in **bold** are explained in the Words to Know section at the back of the book.

Useful Web Sites

Addresses in this book take you to the home pages of Web sites that have information about alligators and crocodiles.

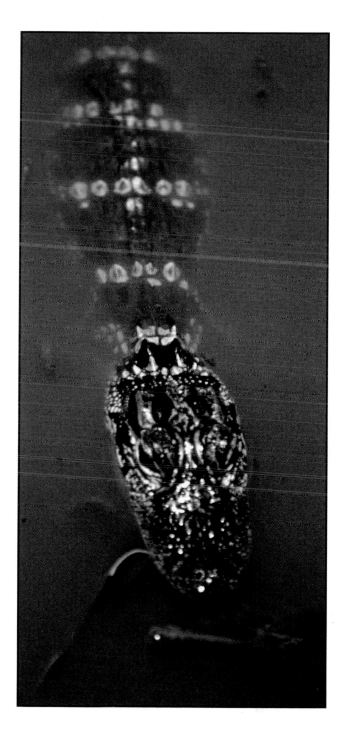

Contents

Meet the Alligator and Crocodile

Alligators and crocodiles belong to a group of animals called reptiles. Reptiles have hard, scaly skin all over their bodies. Snakes, lizards, and turtles are reptiles, too.

Alligators and crocodiles spend part of their time on land and part of their time in rivers or lakes. They are expert swimmers. They stay near the surface of the water so that they can breathe air.

▼ Crocodiles, much like alligators, have very sharp teeth for tearing food.

Alligator and Crocodile Facts

- Alligators and crocodiles eat only meat.
- Alligators and crocodiles have flaps of skin that keep water from getting into their ears.

▲ A crocodile has a long, powerful tail to help it swim through the water.

Fierce Creatures

A crocodile's body is made for chasing, catching, and eating other animals. The crocodile lies very still in the water and waits for its **prey** to come near. Then it leaps out and catches the animal in its huge mouth. An alligator hunts and kills in the same way.

Match the Skulls

1. A gharial has a long, very narrow snout.

2. An alligator has a wide snout.

3. A crocodile has a pointed snout.

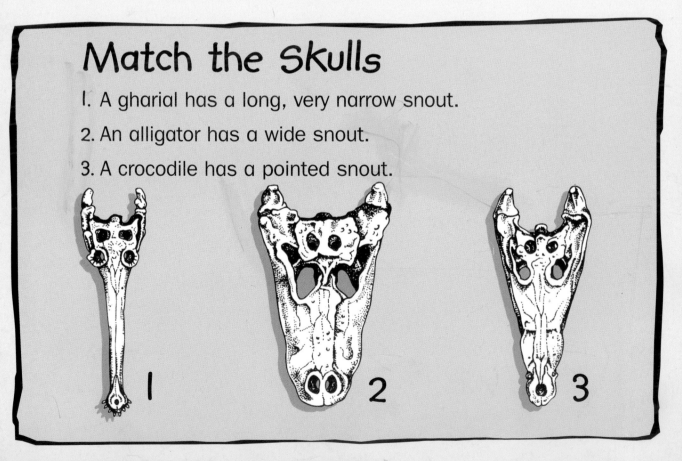

An alligator or crocodile pushes itself through the water with its strong tail.

Nostrils on top of its head let the animal breathe while it hides underwater.

Enormous jaws are lined with sharp teeth for catching and eating prey.

Tough, scaly skin protects the alligator or crocodile from other animals.

Where Do They Live?

Alligators and crocodiles live in hot countries around the world. They cannot make heat inside their bodies, so they need to sunbathe to stay warm.

Alligators and crocodiles are found in lakes, rivers, and **swamps**. They usually hunt for food in the water. When they need to warm up, they climb onto the land.

▼ Alligators and crocodiles live both on land and in water.

Living with Crocodiles

There are many different kinds of animals that live in the same places as crocodiles.

- antelopes
- buffaloes
- fish
- jaguars
- lions
- rhinoceroses
- snakes
- storks
- turtles
- warthogs
- zebras

▲ Alligators and crocodiles like to warm themselves in the sun.

What Do They Eat?

Alligators and crocodiles eat all kinds of small animals, such as birds, fish, frogs, snakes, and turtles. They even eat the babies of other alligators or crocodiles. They swallow small creatures whole.

A large animal, such as a deer or a pig, also makes a tasty meal. The alligator or crocodile drags its prey underwater to drown it, then eats the meat. After feeding, the alligator or crocodile may not eat again for many months.

▼ A crocodile grabs any food it can, even birds such as storks.

What a Meal!

If an alligator or crocodile ate the same kind of food as a human, its meal would be huge.

- 800 fish sticks

- 500 hamburgers

- 400 sausages

- 50 chickens

- 20 turkeys

▲ Alligators and crocodiles like to feast on large animals, such as a wildebeest.

Making Friends

Some alligators and crocodiles like to gather in groups. They mostly sleep, rest, and **bask** in the sun together. When water is difficult to find, they gather around **waterholes**.

Baby alligators and crocodiles often live in families with their mother. She keeps the young reptiles safe from harm. The family may stay together until the young are several years old.

▼ Young alligators stay with their mothers for several years.

Crocodile Talk

Alligators and crocodiles keep in touch with each other by making different kinds of noises.

- They often bellow, or call loudly, to each other.
- They make a noise called a headslap. To do this, an alligator or crocodile lifts its head up, then slaps its mouth onto the surface of the water.

▲ Often, crocodiles will gather in groups to bask in the sun.

Growing Up

A female alligator or crocodile uses plants and mud to build a nest for her family. She lays eggs in the nest and buries them to keep them warm.

Most of the eggs are eaten by birds, lizards, and other animals. Only a few eggs hatch. The tiny **hatchlings** break out of their shells. The mother picks them up in her mouth and carries them to a pond. She takes care of them until they are large enough to look after themselves.

▼ Hatchlings need to be protected from other animals. Very few survive.

Useful Web Sites
http://www.nps.gov/ever/eco/gator.htm
Learn about alligators living in the Everglades by visiting this Web site.

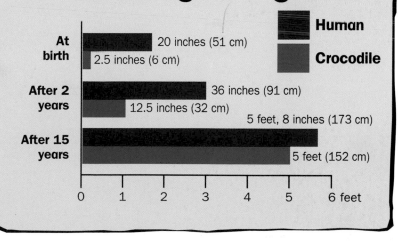

▲ A mother crocodile watches out for her young.

Comparing Lengths

Human
Crocodile

At birth
20 inches (51 cm)
2.5 inches (6 cm)

After 2 years
36 inches (91 cm)
12.5 inches (32 cm)

After 15 years
5 feet, 8 inches (173 cm)
5 feet (152 cm)

0 1 2 3 4 5 6 feet

Enemies

Alligators and crocodiles have tough skin to protect them from hungry **predators**. Only the largest and fiercest animals dare to attack them. Lions may kill crocodiles for food. A lion's sharp teeth can bite through a crocodile's skin.

Some snakes are also dangerous to crocodiles. In South America, a giant snake called an anaconda can wrap itself around a crocodile and squeeze it to death.

▶ Lions can pose a threat to crocodiles.

Putting up a Fight

These animals may fight with crocodiles or kill them for meat.

- hippopotamuses
- jaguars
- leopards
- lions
- rhinoceroses
- tigers

▲ A rhinoceros eats only plants, but it may fight with crocodiles.

Under Threat

Humans are the biggest threat to alligators and crocodiles. People kill the animals and use their skin to make bags, boots, and belts. Some kinds of alligators and crocodiles may die out altogether. There are laws to prevent this from happening.

People harm alligators and crocodiles in other ways, too. They tamper with the rivers and swamps where the animals live. People also **pollute** the water, which makes it dangerous for animals to live there.

▼ Alligators and crocodiles need fresh, clean water to live in.

Useful Web Sites
www.kidsplanet.org/factsheets/
american__crocodile.html
Visit this Web site to learn how to help protect the American crocodile.

What Do You Think?

- Do we need to make clothing from alligator and crocodile skins?

- Should we protect wild alligators and crocodiles, and the places where they live?

▲ For years, people have hunted alligators for their skin.

Myths and Legends

Since early times, people around the world have told stories about crocodiles.

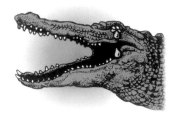

The term "crocodile tears" means pretending to cry. In the past, people thought that crocodiles pretended to cry. When other animals came to see what was wrong, the crocodile would snap them up.

Strange but True

Ancient Egyptians thought that crocodiles made their crops grow well. One of the ancient Egyptian gods had a crocodile head.

Chinese Dragons

Many Chinese myths and stories are about dragons. In some stories, dragons are reptiles with horns, sharp teeth, scaly bodies, and claws. These creatures are much like crocodiles.

▶ Can you tell which parts of a Chinese dragon look like a crocodile?

21

Quiz

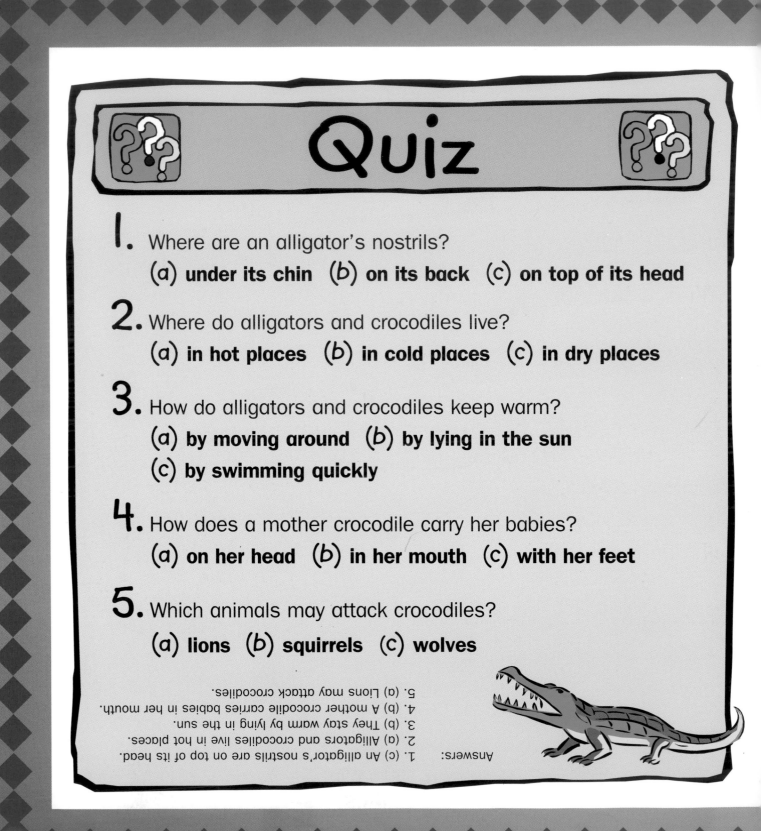

1. Where are an alligator's nostrils?

(a) **under its chin**   (b) **on its back**   (c) **on top of its head**

2. Where do alligators and crocodiles live?

(a) **in hot places**   (b) **in cold places**   (c) **in dry places**

3. How do alligators and crocodiles keep warm?

(a) **by moving around**   (b) **by lying in the sun**
(c) **by swimming quickly**

4. How does a mother crocodile carry her babies?

(a) **on her head**   (b) **in her mouth**   (c) **with her feet**

5. Which animals may attack crocodiles?

(a) **lions**   (b) **squirrels**   (c) **wolves**

Answers:
1. (c) An alligator's nostrils are on top of its head.
2. (a) Alligators and crocodiles live in hot places.
3. (b) They stay warm by lying in the sun.
4. (b) A mother crocodile carries babies in her mouth.
5. (a) Lions may attack crocodiles.

Find out More

To find out more about alligators and crocodiles, visit the Web sites in this book. You can also write to these organizations.

World Wildlife Fund, Canada
Suite 504
90 Eglinton Avenue E.
Toronto, Ontario
M4P 2Z7

Ranger Rick's Nature Club
National Wildlife Federation
8926 Leesburg Pike
Vienna, VA 22184-0001

Words to Know

bask
lie in warmth or sunshine
hatchlings
newly hatched animals
pollute
make very dirty
predators
animals that hunt other animals
for food

prey
an animal that is hunted for food
swamps
places with wet, marshy land
waterholes
ponds or pools where animals come
to drink

Index